touch wood

ALBERT MOBILIO

touch wood

BLACK SQUARE EDITIONS & THE BROOKLYN RAIL

BROOKLYN, NEW YORK 2011

Where no wood is, there the fire goes out.

PROVERBS 26:20

ACKNOWLEDGMENTS

A prose version of "Some Place" appeared in *110 Stories*, edited by Ulrich Baer and published by New York University Press in 2002.

Versions of "Far as Mine Goes," "Circuit Breaks," "Social Struggle," and "We Hold Our Heads High" were published in the electronic journal *Titanic Operas* in 2003.

Versions of "Big Sleeping Job," and "Only Woman in the World" were published in *Lilies & Cannonballs Review* Fall/Winter 2004-2005.

A shorter version of "Letters from Mayhem" was published as an artist's book in collaboration with Roger Andersson by Cabinet Books in 2005.

"I First Read" appeared in *Miracle of Measure: A Festschrift for Gustaf Sobin* published by Talisman House in 2005.

"The Spelled-Out Spark in Rooms" was commissioned by and presented at the Pulitzer Foundation in St. Louis, Missouri, and then published in *The Brooklyn Rail* in 2009.

"Touch Wood" and "Provision" appeared in *Agni Online*, Spring 2010.

"The Whole of It Is Winged" and "Conditional Tense" appeared in *1913: A Journal of Forms* in 2010.

CONTENTS

touch wood

TOUCH WOOD

pillar then pedestal & yes
you want to be saved, not tossed
off, left to wrecks:
wheel's teeth per inch;
wordage over blood pressure;
speed at which cylinders spin;
or nickels enough to fill
his fist, then hers, then how
many times clenched

makes revolution happen,
revolving doors stop. you start
off already unable,
addled even, by proximity
to this or that bull's eye, another
glossy page, one more
instance of giving to get
& what you get is mortal cold
but spit-shined. so being loved

isn't smart; it's lincoln logs,
mortise & tenon,
a kind of compulsion, a cabin
with its curl of smoke.
we lay down housed,
our animal griefs
intact inside such labor.

THE WHOLE OF IT IS WINGED

the whole of it is winged, this science
of speaking about large things
in pocket-size
you do it by letting likeness creep in,
makes me resemble you &
the other way round & it's goodbye
to truth, which
feels quiet at first

then implausibly so
how easily we play this squeezebox,
step wide & bow
to beat the band, so many loves belong
to us, our song is
a perilous thrust, a pistol really,
handheld & in consequence
so much easier to aim

AVERAGE READER

In that vale of beards, my shoes
pried off by propositions
written broken-english-wise.

I was reading out in the yard,
dyslexic sulk in place: How does
the armchair detective discover

who gets curbed by whispers?
Locution will blaze away,
so much so you can't shift pages

out from under whatever sanity
gleams down from lovely, oh
lovely high.

CONDITIONAL TENSE

standing: we was nearly lifelike,
even in the close-ups but how

things modify & where
the middle goes
when the edges fade, well,

that's what cowboys call
surrounded
chill sliver of bright

excitement—quick swigs, stars
on the radio, our body
an anchor amid seas

DECLINE, FALLING

not mere accident if a savage conqueror should

issue from the desert, he sometimes speaks,
becomes more

personal amid the drug
of lovers, first

with exile and afterward his garments
torn and strewn

my discipline relaxes as precipitation
enters streets, dishevels the sun

and every restraint is scorned: an infancy,
this lion's ride when

each hour hangs over their heads
his body secretly

conveyed out, always outwardly
the maxim is a sword, that tyrant

is no more
nourished by irresistible weight, we have

reason to tremble, and then alone

CIRCUIT BREAKS

Humanized
by purest antiquity
I'm quite the choked-up hoax

My arms inclined to climb
so physical to physical
lasts long

enough to rub within
It's dubious, this creature's
stumbling fate: denial is

a prisoner's
lyre

When you look down
from my trusty old ladder
what you see

is really just bait

Chest to chest
whenever you're asked to
There are stages on which you can hide

I'm solo, mesmerized
and very discretely bought

Come on, that skull is perceptibly fake

PROVISION

There could be more: a seed, a speck,
a mud-colored bone. Could be
a conviction,

a scheduled stop, a vividly
depicted shore against which,
a ceaseless beating. Don't ask me

how much I need, how
purposeful I am. Through
a window or in the mail, could be

an escape, a damp footprint
inexplicable on the floor.
Sitting up, standing,

hand in my own hand,
hair on my neck slightly alert —
a bandage, a spoon cool to the touch,

the velocity of figure over ground.
Swarming fans, their loud
imperative mood; strugglers,

climbers, newcomers,
each graced by the novelist's
telling trait & winning way.

There could be more: a confession's
calculated arc of descent, a room cleaned,
the patient having checked out.

Pages learned, ambiguous tints
brought into focus, curtains drawn
as if they could conceal

the decision made in the near dark,
each visible to the other
but not really, not enough.

There could be more: latches
heard while lying in bed;
a photo of soldiers holding ropes

that fills my head,
one afternoon, riding the train,
emptiness as sharply felt as ever.

There could be, might
be, but you can be sure that less
stalks more at every turn.

THIS PRETTY PLEDGE

She sits onstage
so tiltingly wry,
shudders sent
up & down
the aisle from here
to over there

Smart stuff this
beauty vs. art,
agreeing to agree
that a paper cut's
been made by butter
knife & then
count how high
the moon gets
after swallowing
the pill they call
Big Slouch

I'm tied by
my tourniquet;
she's measuring
out a cup
of the kingdom—
a real cheat
this incurable

tension
but wordy
implication only
twists the knot

SOCIAL STRUGGLE

Commandment
breaker, look at you:

bedroom lures and tight-toed shoes

On this sixth day of windshield strain
rise up without a word

Semi-private, semi-circling thoughts,
the season seeps beneath my hat

A head full of clauses when you
talk as if stirring a drink
with your tongue

We're mixing at the mixer
Our brilliant bits ignite

But something in your toolbox tells me
there's going to be a beating

Bone spurs, then greasy noise

I'm what's called a nerve-racking reactor,
a dance-floor mastermind

I want to be ready when the cry goes up

FAR AS MINE GOES

My night watch: night watches me
breezing on a spumy sea of lists

Knotted waves pulled taut as dark
grows large & takes its place

The boatsman yawns, his plot
sketched in leafless scenes

My headache passes overhead,
far along & veiled thus we row

WE HOLD OUR HEADS HIGH

Pretend if you can
that it's last August's fairground,
your conquest amazing
the guys in their work boots.
We're running the show,
a buyer's bonanza,
falling all over ourselves.

Up at the crack, ready to crow,
an hour of sullen, the next
one we're angry.
Her rule is you sock it away
till the weekend
when she rouses herself
to autograph shame.
Inaudible idiom,
she loosens its tendrils
while tightening its sighs.

I wanted to join the impulse
patrol & ride
the sensation of being allowed,
but I'm hearing her sway
in her best-dressed
evasion – I'm over
a barrel & bobbing in vain.

SWING MUSIC

I was doing things
with a ball-peen hammer,
glorious things.
The action just takes you—

from a fearsome brink
you're barreling through:
choosing to grip, fast
twitch in search

of that unlikely dime
to make that call to make
her see how easily
a stocking might be rolled

down a cloudless leg.
Full arm in action, swinging
sings against glass
& glass reacts: breakage is

a kind of bruise—the air
around me aches.

WHAT THE GREAT ONES DO

My lovely intricacies dying
on a soiled vine; my bleak worm eating

away at life. Such vaporous declension
from the normative. The pivot

made, then phrase upon flesh: naked
as a chainsaw whirring

in god's own sun. I am futile,
knowledgeable as every & each.

All quicksilver dew on yellowy pad:
that's what they call persona.

The taste, touch & temperature,
mine from whisker to conundrum's seat.

Watch me break up couplets
with nervy stares or ease from Nessus

venom to burn away your hurt.
I've learned to read the way I write;

but here on the darkling plain, flailing
at these awful stars, this indeed is no lie:

I'm stealing your poem because it's
almost, nearly entirely mine.

HOMAGE TO AN
AVAILABLE LANDSCAPE

Of course the mighty face.
Sand banks, stung with grass.
And the long slur of dusk.

There's the distracted mood –
one as likely to shift as wind.
Perfectibility on some minds;

concupiscence on others.
Certain ideas held high
like flags at homecoming.

That shore, those tides.
Lips all smeared yet she's
even prettier, better prepared

to do *lonely* at an audition.
It's unavoidable, this talk
of what's meant by ascension.

A gardening metaphor curves
meteorological then surgical.
Surprised, she opens her mouth,

the soul's true window.
There are waves; their tendency
to change moods. And again the face.

And the swell of its uppermost,
ever unpronounceable crown.

GUEST LECTURE

And for this hour: the theme
of intention, and how a cup of tea
still tastes like tea even after

bronze-hoofed horses appear
outside, puffed with fame, summer
rain streaming over their backs,

a sight that persuades you
to be selfless, while your lecture
is translated word for word

from a dialect that
nests in a plume of disease...

And for this hour: uses of lurid
externalities, unknown proximities,
and why you can spot

angels in paintings: they look
downright smug
about their immortality

while lordly breath ruffles
their gowns & whatever
god wants, god takes

on a platter, his eyes
rake the back rows for absentees
who think they've heard horns

aloft before
under different, higher ceilings...

And for this hour: our theme
is enchantment, the well-
spring of irresistible fire—veins,

hunger, the sucking soil,
all these mix
in your mouth as you start

with some perception that turns
the trick, your audience
elated as you say *you have died*

as many moments as you have
lived & damn that ghost roams
wide, its heat freshly shed,

the sprawl of its groped-for world
now a greater thing than thee...

DESPITE WHICH SLID

wide of reliable thoughts & emboldened
by my errors as they
        mean something different they often do

when handled on the run, so to speak, a tightened
grip & howdy handshake seals
        the deal; the wrong way of thinking

is always next to the right one, just about to shift
over killing this by killing that & why
        shoulder such happenstance,

each of us flat against the glass, the glass against
this cartesian forest in which we play
        the stranger overly

delighted by our strangeness; you endure this
scrutiny, mind-netted – they watch me, too,
        like a boss who enjoys

his lawnchair: *go sail*, I'm told, but my agility is
insufficient, no easy perch in some
        bird-slung latitude so

it's really only ground covered, the ticking down
of *want*, that dumbfuck courage
        needed to overflow a mile

GOWNED AND SPOKEN

can you bear to look she's such
almighty gowned & solves

puzzles by bending pieces to fit
her naturally occurring strife

wasn't near as spacious
as that attic where deepening

goes to hide its depths
intellect's defeat, a waste

we activate ourselves
no more splash & peach-soft hips

that glow is gone, we're merely
steady, elegiac now

KIN

He's my brother, but I made
him up: Someone older, wiser.
The story I told was detailed,
sounded quite credible:

He did physics, investigating
shoe scuffs; he made California his
island home; he wore
silent style & average ties;
he played Army, shouting "*towz, towz!*"
the bullets as they ricocheted;

he married, very lovely & nieces
in blue shorts, ankle deep in pond;
he spoke in slant
rhymes & never let his hat alone,
always sharpening its crease.
That panzer couch commander

I talked so much about – Orville
to my Wilbur. No kidding,
it's a fact: I bet he remembers you
& he might even know me, too.

BIG SLEEPING JOB

Laughter seeks its own lament
and little old misery blooms in its sack

I'm just a lonesome babe in the wood
You know me so throw me on a couch

Fragments of flaws and pieces of that,
you could make a tough road smoothly go

Each cloud hauls its portion of gray,
birds on branches like jittery phones

Hesitate then ominous gust
Avenging the bruise, I dash around town

spending quarters you find in my couch
What a gimmick I've got on a leash

THE NOTHING NEW

some deal this: struck dumb,
my three maybe four ideas

under scrutiny, which isn't
very desirable

for anyone who would
rather skim than dive,

brake while others forward
scroll. deferment:

not misfortune but a plan —
making faces that pass

for feelings, not saying
what comes to mind, reckon

instead the aftermath of
please or *the fan's too loud*

or *I'm with you now,*
this way slipping through flight

delays, off-pitch recitals,
remissions, feints made & failed,

all the while nothing, truth told,
ever so mineral

hard as the falter
any comma is.

ONLY WOMAN IN THE WORLD

Like you I'm at the window too,
dexterity filling its private pool

How red this redness gets

I watch you just beginning to
Your learning curve is sound

Why not make me make
you slide this way

A little applied to your neck,
a little more

dampens your wrists

This silent-film scene is
fractioned

by blinds—

I read your lips as you groom
each page

Cast-off sighs, blossoms
on the floor

OUT PAST THE POINT

The Narrows, lauded in distant climes – spangled
sleeves of heightened exposition

I told the pharmacist I was ready for my minus sign,
ready for my paper's marks

The solution, he said, take two spoons' worth,
before this heat & after

you've worked the last
grains of sand from your shoes

Bottles afloat, bodies out there lounging, many
milks of kindness raining down

We slip on rocks; we choir these twists & aughts,
but I still take your not enough

& leave another stupid message on your phone
The sky feels hard, hours too,

such vast abrupt – a mess of weeds, a sudden mind
where all my war is done

MEMORIZED

there's very good cause to feel
miniature:

at the kitchen table he's opening an envelope
certain things about the stove
are intimated

sly bifurcation, this
blown-down door goes south:

he starts with a pencil & ends
with a future; the difficult path of self-
improvement

drowsy, drowsy grows & them
that on such sofa nod:

what a way to say he's been the ruin
of himself: born & brought up
to lay his hands upon

oars across days — the most
natural locomotion:

a history of his treatments:
some used wire, others whatever could
be torn from whole

a thousand's
thousand spies:

this drawer, that cup: he washes,
then shelves —

brought round & banged upon
by idiot earth:

remember a storm & paper scattered?
the day after, grass flattened
as if by stone

an active Spirit, the skull-
bone proclaims its pure immediacy:

he holds an unstruck match,
those lives outside & atoms,
even, among

EVERYDAY ERRORS IN SYLLABICATION

read aloud,
focus on the first *s*.

the letter's
in its envelope; my bad news
too roughly hung.

go hide away
a common world. never
rhyme *for*
with *endure* &

sometimes
you must wait a bit.

no longer am I
compelled to cling: having
nothing to do
with parades

(though there's a tremor
throughout this choice).

my raining part gives
way to dry as permissible
regains then stalls.

I find access
difficult, caught up
here in commission

of one or another wrong.

read aloud
such remotes
as will be reached.

I FIRST READ

for Gustaf Sobin

I first read this body's breath is made from the pause
    taken just as you reach for but then leave
a door unopened, or leave
   today's newspaper folded, or
      begin to explain why saying
         next to nothing
   is near enough an epic as saying all

I first read this body's breath is drawn through grass,
    across a field; the rain-wet slope is a verb, rocks
and stones ellipses, and each muddy cleft a dash
      that bridges with sparked
         expectation what other-
   wise would snag on earth's rough touch

I first read this body's breath is blown across
heights as – having found a fissure
in the wall of a ruined house – a weed might split
weak mortar to form a fisted tuft
   of leaves that holds
the quarried blocks and prayers pressed into place

I first read this body's breath is fed by living
        song, which we hear as an inward
tending part of speech even as it presses
                    out against the farthest trees
                        and blue-streaked ridge
        where mind sheds sound as if its words can reach

this body's breath I read is made of air, unbroken air

THE SPELLED-OUT SPARK IN ROOMS

for *Dan Flavin*

The mind's eye begins with atmosphere & islets
of dust. Sorts out the various

kinds of dark—the blue-black of casual doom,
the humid shade collecting under bridges

or the charcoal hue that settles
in hospital rooms after visiting hours. Beamish

to lusterless, satellite to blacktop's skid.
Every fleck a sun, every sun a dial to be turned—

II

On the verge of palpable: that's where
the mind's eye begins.

Even as a lamp gives off heat, weird laws
govern just how much (they bend

when necessary; even the gods
open windows for want of a breeze): glare

of signage, its flicker urges us somewhere
warmer than mere night.

III

The atomists, we're told, believed
in an *imago* that vision peeled off, say,

an orange; the *optick*, then, a circuit self-
sufficient in a bodiless world.

But pictures don't make you wince
at noon—lay out in its blaze or hide

among big rocks, you're still magnified
within sunlight's inelastic speed.

IV

So there are rays. Strong ones, others
only splinters—a flashlight's shaky beam spies

out a furnace gauge or palms press eyelids:
starry zone, particles of nowhere.

v

Take hold of useful tools, eggbeaters, mallets,
and slingshots – things from cartoons. Things

thin as painted air. Sensation's cloud
inhaled through blue, green, red straws leaning

in the corner feigning stealth. *We're all
around this campfire singing.*

VI

In a television's stuttered glow — revenge
carried out by a woman wearing

a towel; a Spanish boy kneeling in an attic.
Stories seek geometries — column,

frame, fenestra — through which phosphor
moves discontentedly, ever more perishable.

If the passageway's impassable you'll slouch
instead in its fabricated dusk.

VII

A sparkling disco ball or Descartes peering
through an ox's eye. Nothing more

than vibration, sunrise failing
to dismantle the old fort. Mirrors mirror

what's unconcealed: daybreak streaming
only as far as the cord allows.

VIII

If a sentence moved rapidly as sight, its verb
would be a tweezer-size pyre

consuming the word *traverse*. Lightning made
smooth on paper. Silver, silver-true,

an instrument is launched
in the chromosphere. Cigar-shaped, scissor-bright

& alive as a moon, a dashboard, as frequency
is often monumental, always sentient.

IX

Fluorescent detonation at your feet.

Shapes on the valley floor, indistinct
as exhalation. The eye surveys –

illumes – in these woods, on a patio, by the bed
articulates prescription bottles,

a comb, an empty glass – and this
light is the deed, the suffering of darkness.

LETTERS FROM MAYHEM

His inmost thoughts are discussed at nightfall,
in manual alphabet, by darkly gesticulating trees.

VLADIMIR NABOKOV, "Signs and Symbols"

amen)

I was motor-minded
from the very first. Big,

even bigger gears round rounding

in my brainpan. Among the steep-laced
boys, I hung out

& slackly combed. Summers
were years, years an unclockable

sky under which we learned to swerve.

before was once)

We sewed teeth into shoplifted myths,
but my urge was a crowd that couldn't

fit through their needle's eye.

cede)

A disguise as thin as a playing card. Worn when
you're calm as only

a decoy is. As when paradise is
a metallic taste in the back of your throat.

That's when you'll find
me in a singing state: fizzy gunning of bass

guitar grown loud between
these bleary weirds.

deeds done)

In the temple of human reduction, I took up
the pen of nature yet no one searched.

That night on the floor of the visitors'
dugout, I lay sick, my stomach dry. And still

I went unsought.

erase, erase)

Why no headlights
in our blindness? In such sleeps I'm beguiled

by this childish yet radiant dread.
The current burns

the wire; a river schemes against its banks.
And I'm knocked

headlong by the name I call myself.

effable)

No mental chasm here. This is what you get
when you've got it coming. She knows

so many shortcuts — like the one behind the mall
where you climb the fence by the U-Haul lot.

I've been with her
on roofs and on the high rocks. Wind ballooning

our skinny jackets, the moonlight
gone dirty through our tears.

geographed)

Out back of a backfence
world, so dusty

a fuck was we.

ancient civ)

If I look when she warns me not to, I get to see
how she calibrates

each stain. I'm gang-planked
on her ark, sent

out into a weather of doused torches.

icon steady)

We got hammered in the spirit world.
Everything that's known

can be found in any single sentence yet still
we swooned to a whiff of Thai stick. Tube-tops

at the barbecue. And night
was a wet nurse to our stars.

jade)

French inhaling, collars wreathed in cultish smoke.
Dice decide the matter.

I kid you not the rush is good. Chance isn't
a sign but instead it's my hands

held against—I can breathe
between spread fingers. A different day,

& maybe I'm not this tame.

cave kept)

Like weeds, we crept
out of rifts. Ornaments of decay. As primed

for sun as for a blade.

lull)

There is this need to hold closely.
But first you must unwind & straighten

out the facts. Make sure that seeming
can be trusted, isn't just tactile

insinuation. I want to be welcome
at the door, even if I can't tender

the password, my tongue tied
on the letter "Say."

membrane)

The days were aerial, the towns
erratic. There's nothing we won't sell

or trade to wheel away again: perspiring
beneath the chemical
glance, our whole capsule dissolving,

dissolving.

end over)

Fitfully blamed, beaten
over silly rules, I rummaged through

the schoolhouse.
Continuous is really just telling; we seek

addition, seek
our human wish reborn.

ode)

In the alley there are wondrous, subtle
planets. Vinyl sides

played down to crosshatched static.
To steer is to be vast &

to be thrown loose; what revolves
is revealed

to be what moves best: who doesn't
please themselves first, then leftovers later

for the scurrying host of sorrowful cast.

peaking now)

As good as poured when she spills her glass

& then mine on purpose – our boozy theme
immersed in blame. We're compressed,

minute joys done in the bleacher seats;
we trade the photos that come

with our wallets & how slips
from me my combination?

cue strings, lights)

Etcetera's incision now
released across the dial. Listen in

for the ferocity, the purgative
spike: girls in reckless

glow, someone pithy scores
unbowed.

ardently)

The prophet is plain, no eye shadow
or shadows anywhere; she's prepared

for useless expectation. Lovers crouch
inside a cinder-block enclosure, warm place

between them, but destined to be pried away
by familiarity, by being

pitiable, inhabitable.

yes)

That's monkey time and already
we're set for menthol glide.

We're greedy eats & our mental maneuvers
end properly, gongs

clamoring. My prize is yours & necessities

unfurl in window dark.

tease me)

Resembles a good chase or the way that Chevy
peels off asphalt or any other

method of procession – my tethered course,
my hymnal shut, all as fast

as could falls headlong into can't.

used you)

I cannot remove this lamplight, its smudged
tent spreads over me & nothing

else could shelter my slyness. Many make
lists but

much too complete these days: we've blown
whispers into shouts, sticks

into forests. And how ruin
creeps over

a multitude of single things.

vis-à-vis)

Ruminate then kick the safety from self-love's gun;

you start to forget when you learn to leave. Let's not
make too much

of our rendezvous in this floorless life.

double view)

Pretty are these fears; they're also armed.
We bite into our second-guess.

Which way goes her magic?
Back to that gloomy spoof,

a home movie starring the meek who grin
shit-eating grins

while they inherit one more pearly earth?

exalted)

In that rustling, gauze-lit bower, curious
man that he was, the bold scout

unburdened himself: her palm sufficiently
rounded, she tested him, kissed as though

borrowing from a thief: good phoning
to be had in the hallway, under

bulb's crazy flicker where he fell hard
to realize her timing

was the same as his, sprung up from
his own loamy patch.

wise, word to)

Wasn't a physical specimen, wasn't visibly
fledged – but what revival

to be felt while working this needle. I patch
where torn, where bloodied.

But digression makes it hard to see
what my fingers actually do, to operate

fluently, as free as mind can be, made up
with whatever thread is left.

zeroing in)

My thorny problem: everything is difficult as
I am driven by purely

directional noise but cannot match
sensation with acts,

cannot undergo grand effects. To walk through
this day, over that pavement,

wherever the sun cloaks semblance – then
come to a standstill, perhaps

poolside, where I hope to be desirous & able
to bequeath something

momentary, fully tuned.

SOME PLACE,
SAME PLACE

Under this
roof distance is
made small;
a door swings wide,
no one passes through.
That was where
it happened:
we were standing,
or nodding, or
I saw myself
pass by,
face fractioned
in car windows.

You were walking,
or sleeping
in, or we met
at the coffee place.
I was reading alone,
you were in town,
or at home turning
on the radio.
You thought this
is that place where
you find yourself
lately, with

shouting
between buildings,
Apaches on the ridge,
eyes peeled for wagons.

We learned facts —
a field of cut grass,
broken glass;
something hidden
behind the sofa;
something else now
lodged inside the sky.
You felt hours
shoulder their way
into space.
I was telling you
about what I saw
in car windows,
about how we live
as if, and
as if.

HEAVEN WILL

receive such offerings: tapering toward,
this one rides a pronouncement-heavy moon,

or on television that vatican black tear
as if indecision were nothing more than leakage;

this rosy swirl across the river so thick you can't
see whether it's chimney, pit, or engine

kicked into life, so many — seasonal,
medicinal, industrial — and then lungfuls over-

worked, our exhalation never done: rise
we rise, these ashes in our hair, blue yonder

shaking free, the wind voluminous
with murmur & lift

ROUNDING OFF TO THE NEAREST ZERO

The day he died turned out to be a convenient time for that sort of thing. When someone dies, there's much to do; many details to look after. This takes up an awful lot of time so if he died a few weeks before or a few weeks after that day, I would have been sorely pressed. But, like I said, he died rather neatly schedule-wise.

I rented a car, mid-size, with electric adjustable seats. The drive is a long one and with the traffic you get on the turnpike, the comfort is worth a few extra dollars. Driving, or at least driving alone, is, I've always found, conducive to thinking. The sense of forward motion, the calf's calibrated flexing, the purposeful grip of the wheel combine, it seems, to concentrate the mind. The first thought that occurred to me as I maneuvered into the passing lane and settled in at a good clip for the duration was to reflect on why my first thought, my very first reaction upon hearing the news on the phone had been, well, that this is a convenient time, a good time for this to happen. Most likely I didn't articulate such words to myself. But the word *good* was somewhere in that moment, hovering in the thick swirl of feelings.

The caller, the woman who had watched him succumb to a heart attack, who said he was laughing and talking one minute and lifeless, mouth agape the next, said it was a "good death," meaning quick and painless; there had been no time for him to brood upon the event. A good death. So that word was indeed spoken. Was in my head. Her positive, if not glowing, appraisal invited some sort of enlargement on my part. It was a good death, she said, and I compounded this fortune by judging it to have occurred at a good time, at least for me. Again, maybe I didn't say that word, but there was my relieved exhalation, the feeling that a difficult thing had gone off without a hitch, that there would be no unmanageable repercussions.

And so I considered this, considered my general approbation of his good death at a good time. I changed lanes and pulled aside a huge truck carrying several shiny pickup trucks. All the lanes were crowded but the traffic was still moving. So here was my first thought on this long drive alone in a rental car and already I was aware of just how long I would be sitting where I was sitting, hands on the wheel, purposefully.

I felt around the dashboard for the radio knob and noted the time on the digital display as well as my speed. A quick calculation yielded a figure, the number of hours until I arrived at his house. I thought about that number and recalculated based on averaging three miles an hour faster. I did this again using a different speed. And again, and several times after that. I cracked the window enough to hear that tearing sound you hear in a fast-moving car. I would be getting there, I concluded, with time to spare, one way or another.

ALBERT MOBILIO is the recipient of a Whiting Writers' Award. His work has appeared in Harper's, the Village Voice, Grand Street, Black Clock, Bomb, Cabinet, Talisman, and Tin House. Books of poetry include Bendable Siege, The Geographics, and Me with Animal Towering. He is an assistant professor of literary studies at the New School's Eugene Lang College and is an editor of Bookforum.